Francis Frith's
Edinburgh

Photographic Memories

Francis Frith's
Edinburgh

Revised edition of original work by

Clive Hardy

FRITH
BOOK Co

First published in the United Kingdom in 1998 by
by WBC Ltd

Revised paperback edition published in the United Kingdom in 2000 by
Frith Book Company Ltd

Paperback Edition 1998
ISBN 1-85937-193-0

Reprinted in Hardback 2001
ISBN 1-85937-404-2

British Library Cataloguing in Publication Data

Francis Frith's Edinburgh
Clive Hardy

Frith Book Company Ltd
Frith's Barn, Teffont,
Salisbury, Wiltshire SP3 5QP
Tel: +44 (0) 1722 716 376
Email: info@francisfrith.co.uk
www.francisfrith.co.uk

Printed and bound in Great Britain

AS WITH ANY HISTORICAL DATABASE THE FRITH ARCHIVE IS CONSTANTLY BEING CORRECTED AND IMPROVED
AND THE PUBLISHERS WOULD WELCOME INFORMATION ON OMISSIONS OR INACCURACIES

Contents

Francis Frith: *Victorian Pioneer*

FRANCIS FRITH, Victorian founder of the world-famous photographic archive, was a complex and multitudinous man. A devout Quaker and a highly successful Victorian businessman, he was both philosophic by nature and pioneering in outlook.

By 1855 Francis Frith had already established a wholesale grocery business in Liverpool, and sold it for the astonishing sum of £200,000, which is the equivalent today of over £15,000,000. Now a multi-millionaire, he was able to indulge his passion for travel. As a child he had pored over travel books written by early explorers, and his fancy and imagination had been stirred by family holidays to the sublime mountain regions of Wales and Scotland. 'What a land of spirit-stirring and enriching scenes and places!' he had written. He was to return to these scenes of grandeur in later years to 'recapture the thousands of vivid and tender memories', but with a different purpose. Now in his thirties, and captivated by the new science of photography, Frith set out on a series of pioneering journeys to the Nile regions that occupied him from 1856 until 1860.

Intrigue and Adventure

He took with him on his travels a specially-designed wicker carriage that acted as both dark-room and sleeping chamber. These far-flung journeys were packed with intrigue and adventure. In his life story, written when he was sixty-three, Frith tells of being held captive by bandits, and of fighting 'an awful midnight battle to the very point of surrender with a deadly pack of hungry, wild dogs'. Sporting flowing Arab costume, Frith arrived at Akaba by camel seventy years before Lawrence, where he encountered 'desert princes and rival sheikhs, blazing with jewel-hilted swords'.

During these extraordinary adventures he was assiduously exploring the desert regions bordering the Nile and patiently recording the antiquities and peoples with his camera. He was the first photographer to venture beyond the sixth cataract. Africa was still the mysterious 'Dark Continent', and Stanley and Livingstone's historic meeting was a decade into the future. The conditions for picture taking confound belief. He laboured for hours in his wicker dark-room in the sweltering heat of the desert, while the volatile chemicals fizzed dangerously in their trays. Often he was forced to work in remote tombs and caves where conditions were cooler. Back in London he exhibited his photographs and was 'rapturously cheered' by members of the Royal Society. His reputation as a photographer was made overnight. An eminent modern historian has likened their impact on the population of the time to that on our own generation of the first photographs taken on the surface of the moon.

Venture of a Life-Time

Characteristically, Frith quickly spotted the opportunity to create a new business as a specialist publisher of photographs. He lived in an era of immense and sometimes violent change. For the poor in the early part of Victoria's reign work was a drudge and the hours long, and people had precious little free time to enjoy themselves. Most had no transport other than a cart or gig at their disposal, and had not travelled far beyond the

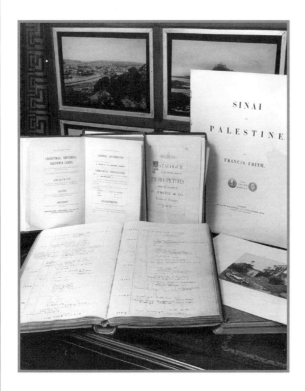

boundaries of their own town or village. However, by the 1870s, the railways had threaded their way across the country, and Bank Holidays and half-day Saturdays had been made obligatory by Act of Parliament. All of a sudden the ordinary working man and his family were able to enjoy days out and see a little more of the world.

With characteristic business acumen, Francis Frith foresaw that these new tourists would enjoy having souvenirs to commemorate their days out. In 1860 he married Mary Ann Rosling and set out with the intention of photographing every city, town and village in Britain. For the next thirty years he travelled the country by train and by pony and trap, producing fine photographs of seaside resorts and beauty spots that were keenly bought by millions of Victorians. These prints were painstakingly pasted into family albums and pored over during the dark nights of winter, rekindling precious memories of summer excursions.

The Rise of Frith & Co

Frith's studio was soon supplying retail shops all over the country. To meet the demand he gathered about him a small team of photographers, and published the work of independent artist-photographers of the calibre of Roger Fenton and Francis Bedford. In order to gain some understanding of the scale of Frith's business one only has to look at the catalogue issued by Frith & Co in 1886: it runs to some 670 pages, listing not only many thousands of views of the British Isles but also many photographs of most European countries, and China, Japan, the USA and

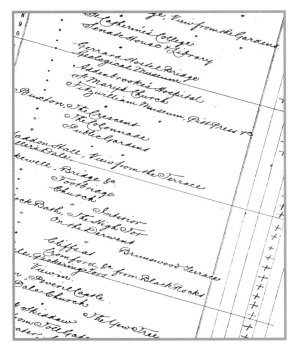

Canada – note the sample page shown above from the hand-written *Frith & Co* ledgers detailing pictures taken. By 1890 Frith had created the greatest specialist photographic publishing company in the world, with over 2,000 outlets – more than the combined number that Boots and WH Smith have today! The picture on the right shows the *Frith & Co* display board at Ingleton in the Yorkshire Dales. Beautifully constructed with mahogany frame and gilt inserts, it could display up to a dozen local scenes.

Postcard Bonanza

The ever-popular holiday postcard we know today took many years to develop. In 1870 the Post Office issued the first plain cards, with a pre-printed stamp on one face. In 1894 they allowed other publishers' cards to be sent through the mail with an attached adhesive halfpenny stamp. Demand grew rapidly, and in 1895 a new size of postcard was permitted called the court card, but there was little room for illustration. In 1899, a year after Frith's death, a new card measuring 5.5 x 3.5 inches became the standard format, but it was not until 1902 that the divided back came into being, with address and message on one face and a full-size illustration on the other. *Frith & Co* were in the vanguard of postcard development, and Frith's sons Eustace and Cyril continued their father's monumental task, expanding the number of views offered to the public and recording more and more places in Britain, as the coasts and countryside were opened up to mass travel.

Francis Frith died in 1898 at his villa in Cannes, his great project still growing. The archive he created continued in business for another seventy years. By 1970 it contained over a third of a million pictures of 7,000 cities, towns and villages. The massive photographic record Frith has left to us stands as a living monument to a special and very remarkable man.

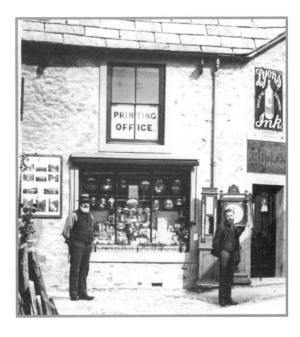

Frith's Archive: *A Unique Legacy*

FRANCIS FRITH'S legacy to us today is of immense significance and value, for the magnificent archive of evocative photographs he created provides a unique record of change in 7,000 cities, towns and villages throughout Britain over a century and more. Frith and his fellow studio photographers revisited locations many times down the years to update their views, compiling for us an enthralling and colourful pageant of British life and character.

We tend to think of Frith's sepia views of Britain as nostalgic, for most of us use them to conjure up memories of places in our own lives with which we have family associations. It often makes us forget that to Francis Frith they were records of daily life as it was actually being lived in the cities, towns and villages of his day. The Victorian age was one of great and often bewildering change for ordinary people, and though the pictures evoke an impression of slower times, life was as busy and hectic as it is today.

We are fortunate that Frith was a photographer of the people, dedicated to recording the minutiae of everyday life. For it is this sheer wealth of visual data, the painstaking chronicle of changes in dress, transport, street layouts, buildings, housing, engineering and landscape that captivates us so much today. His remarkable images offer us a powerful link with the past and with the lives of our ancestors.

Today's Technology

Computers have now made it possible for Frith's many thousands of images to be accessed almost instantly. In the Frith archive today, each photograph is carefully 'digitised' then stored on a CD Rom. Frith archivists can locate a single photograph amongst thousands within seconds. Views can be catalogued and sorted under a variety of categories of place and content to the immediate benefit of researchers.

Inexpensive reference prints can be created for them at the touch of a mouse button, and a wide range of books and other printed materials assembled and published for a wider, more general readership - in the next twelve months over a hundred Frith local history titles will be published! The day-to-day workings of the archive are very different from how they were in Francis Frith's time: imagine the herculean task of sorting through eleven tons of glass negatives as Frith had to do to locate a particular

THE FRANCIS FRITH COLLECTION
Photographic publishers since 1860

| HOME | PHOTO SEARCH | BOOKS | PORTFOLIO | GALLERY | | MY CART |
| Products | History | Other Collections | Contact us | Help? |

your town,
your village

365,000
photographs of 7,000 towns and villages, taken between 1860 & 1970.

The Frith Archive
The Frith Archive is the remarkable legacy of its energetic and visionary founder. Today, the Frith archive is the only nationally important archive of its kind still in private ownership.

The Collection is world-renowned for the extraordinary quality of its images.

The Gallery
This month The Frith Gallery features images from "Frith's Egypt".

the FRITHgallery

News...
Image update complete.
An additional 5,000 images have been added and the quality of all images has now been improved.

Sample Chapters avaliable.
The first selection of sample chapters from the Frith Book Co.'s extensive range is now available. All are offered in Pdf format for easy downloading and viewing.

explore
FRITH
Search thousands of photographs from one of the worlds' great archives.

Town search
GO

County search
Select a county
GO

See Frith at www.francisfrith.co.uk

sequence of pictures! Yet the archive still prides itself on maintaining the same high standards of excellence laid down by Francis Frith, including the painstaking cataloguing and indexing of every view.

It is curious to reflect on how the internet now allows researchers in America and elsewhere greater instant access to the archive than Frith himself ever enjoyed. Many thousands of individual views can be called up on screen within seconds on one of the Frith internet sites, enabling people living continents away to revisit the streets of their ancestral home town, or view places in Britain where they have enjoyed holidays. Many overseas researchers welcome the chance to view special theme selections, such as transport, sports, costume and ancient monuments.

We are certain that Francis Frith would have heartily approved of these modern developments in imaging techniques, for he himself was always working at the very limits of Victorian photographic technology.

The Value of the Archive Today

Because of the benefits brought by the computer, Frith's images are increasingly studied by social historians, by researchers into genealogy and ancestory, by architects, town planners, and by teachers and schoolchildren involved in local history projects.

In addition, the archive offers every one of us an opportunity to examine the places where we and our families have lived and worked down the years. Highly successful in Frith's own era, the archive is now, a century and more on, entering a new phase of popularity.

The Past in Tune with the Future

Historians consider the Francis Frith Collection to be of prime national importance. It is the only archive of its kind remaining in private ownership and has been valued at a million pounds. However, this figure is now rapidly increasing as digital technology enables more and more people around the world to enjoy its benefits.

Francis Frith's archive is now housed in an historic timber barn in the beautiful village of Teffont in Wiltshire. Its founder would not recognize the archive office as it is today. In place of the many thousands of dusty boxes containing glass plate negatives and an all-pervading odour of photographic chemicals, there are now ranks of computer screens. He would be amazed to watch his images travelling round the world at unimaginable speeds through network and internet lines.

The archive's future is both bright and exciting. Francis Frith, with his unshakeable belief in making photographs available to the greatest number of people, would undoubtedly approve of what is being done today with his lifetime's work. His photographs, depicting our shared past, are now bringing pleasure and enlightenment to millions around the world a century and more after his death.

Linlithgow

Situated approximately half-way between
Stirling and Edinburgh, Linlithgow became an
important and favourite royal residence.
During the wars with the English, the town
and its castle were subject to siege and
counter-siege. At Lent in 1314 the English took
Linlithgow by blocking the fall of its portcullis
with hay-carts. Edward II hurried through the
town on his way to Dunbar and the safety of a
ship, following his defeat at Bannockburn.

Linlithgow Palace 1897 39155
The last Scottish national parliament was held here
in 1646. Oliver Cromwell lived at the palace for several months following the Battle of Dunbar in
September 1650.

◀ **Linlithgow Palace, On the South Shore of Linlithgow Loch 1897**
39154
Mary, Queen of Scots was born here in 1542, and Prince Charles Edward Stuart stayed here in 1745. The palace is thought to have been burnt down accidentally in 1746 by some of General Hawley's troops.

◀ **Linlithgow Palace, from the Boat Station 1897** 39153
King David I built the first manor house at Linlithgow, and the church of St Michael next to it. In 1301, Edward Longshanks set about rebuilding and heavily fortifying the palace, and it was held by the English until the autumn of 1313.

▼ **Linlithgow Palace, The Quadrangle 1897**
39156
The Royal apartments were situated on the west side of the quadrangle. Queen Margaret's Bower is where her majesty kept vigil while James IV fought at Flodden.

◀ **Linlithgow Palace, St Michael's Church 1897** 39158
Founded by David I in the 12th century, the church was rebuilt about 300 years later.

Linlithgow, The Cross Well 1897 39157
This well, with its thirteen water jets, is a reconstruction of an earlier one destroyed by Oliver Cromwell's troops.
On 23 January 1570, Regent Moray was shot as he rode through Linlithgow. The assassin hid in a house belonging to John Hamilton, Archbishop of St Andrews. Moray's friends hanged Hamilton at Stirling in 1571. They did not go to the expense of a trial.

Queensferry

Queensferry lies on the south shore of the Firth of Forth. South Queensferry and its counterpart North Queensferry are said have been so-named because Queen Margaret crossed the Forth at this point on her way to Dunfermline.

The Forth Railway Bridge c1890 558
Designed by Sir John Fowler and Sir Benjamin Baker, the Forth Bridge cost £3,000,000 to build. Of the workforce of 4,500 men, 57 were killed in work-related accidents.

The Forth Bridge 1897 39142
Construction of the bridge commenced in November 1882. The first test trains ran from January 1890, and the official opening took place on 4 March 1890.

The Forth Bridge 1897 39141
The bridge is more than over 2,760 yards long, including the approach viaducts, giving a clear headway at high water of 150 ft. The steel towers stand 360 ft high and are supported on granite piers. The deepest foundations are 88 ft below high water.

The View from North Queensferry 1897 39144
Following the opening of the Forth Bridge, the North British Railway Co decided that they could dispense with their ferry services. Accordingly, the licences for the Forth and the Tay were transferred to David Wilson & Sons.

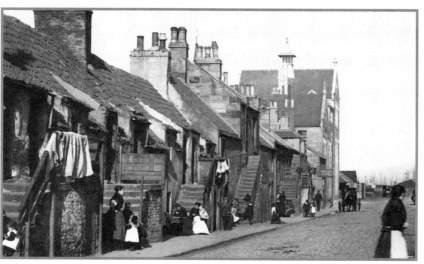

◄ **Newhaven, Fishermen's Cottages 1897** 39137
The fishermen's wives were known for their costumes, which are thought to have had associations with the community's Scandinavian origins. The women also had their own cries when selling fish: 'Caller Herrin' (fresh herrings) and 'Caller Ou' (fresh oysters).

◄ **Newhaven, The Harbour 1897** 39139
The original population of Newhaven was probably of Dutch and Scandinavian origin. For generations the people rarely moved out of their own community, keeping their traditions and customs alive.

Newhaven

This small fishing port was founded by James IV in about 1500. A shipyard and ropeworks were established for the construction of warships.

► **Newhaven, The Harbour from Hawthornden 1897**
39138
In about 1512, one of the biggest warships then in existence was fitting out at Newhaven. She was 'The Great Michael; she was 240 ft long, and carried a crew of 420 and 1,000 soldiers. The mighty warship was one of the units despatched by James IV to assist the French against Henry VIII.

Edinburgh

Edinburgh became Scotland's capital without ceremony more than 500 years ago when James II decided to hold his parliament in the town. Edinburgh (Old Town) was quite small, consisting of only a few hundred houses huddled in close proximity to the eastern side of the Castle. Just when Edinburgh was founded is open to speculation. The name is thought to be derived from 'Edwin's burgh'; Edwin was an early 7th-century king of Northumbria. At that time, Northumbria was all-powerful. Its territory extended from the Forth to the Humber, and Edwin is known to have fortified a part of the area occupied by the present castle. He also encouraged a civilian settlement nearby. Under David I, Edinburgh was a royal burgh, which brought with it a number of trading privileges. In David's day, church and state were interlinked; it was David who re-introduced monasticism back into Scotland.

Edinburgh, John Knox's House 1897 39125
This view shows the lower reach of the High Street looking towards Canongate. The building immediately behind the lamp standard is known as John Knox's house. Dating from the 16th century, the house is said to have been built by Mary, Queen of Scots' goldsmith. Just how long Knox lived here is open to debate.

David granted tracts of land and gave vast amounts of money to the greater glory of God, encouraging Benedictines, Cistercians and most of all Augustinians, to found religious houses. The legend goes that David was out hunting when he was attacked by an infuriated stag. He was saved from certain death by the interposition of a miraculous cross. In thanks, and as a penance for hunting on a holy day, David founded an abbey at Holyrood. Despite the foundation of a great abbey, much of Edinburgh's early history appears to revolve around the castle and the fortunes of the monarchy. Henry VIII was desperate for his son Edward, aged five, to be married to the infant Queen Mary. Scotland at that time was under the governorship of James, 2nd Earl of Arran, who was a Protestant. Through argument, coercion, and downright bribery, Arran persuaded the Scottish parliament to agree to the match, and it was ratified in two treaties at Holyrood in August 1543. But Scotland, as so often in the past, was in turmoil.

Mary of Guise, the infant Queen's mother, was against the wedding; she had the backing of a number of nobles and the Catholic Church. For some reason, Arran suddenly changed faiths and sides, and the infant was crowned Queen of the Scots. Henry was not impressed. In May 1544, an English invasion force arrived off Newhaven. Edinburgh fell to the troops of the Earl of Hertford, though the castle managed to hold out. Hertford burnt Holyroodhouse and the Old Town.

The following year, Hertford was back in Scotland, burning five market towns, sacking 243 villages, and laying waste to crops. Edward was destined not marry the Queen of Scots. He died in 1553 and was succeeded by his Catholic sister. The young Scottish queen was married to Francois, Dauphin of France, an act that was to establish the Auld Alliance. The marriage lasted two years. By 1560 Francois too was dead, and Mary had returned to Scotland.

Edinburgh, Holyrood Palace, King Charles's Bedroom 1897
39173

Edinburgh, Holyrood Palace and Arthur's Seat 1897 39168
Extensive alterations to the palace were undertaken between 1670 and 1679 by Sir William Bruce, the king's Surveyor in Scotland. The strong French influence in Sir William's designs reflected Charles II's passion for things Gallic.

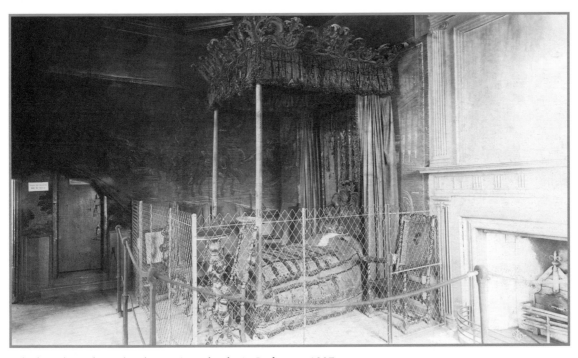

Edinburgh, Holyrood Palace, King Charles's Bedroom 1897 39172
A fence and rope guard the old feathered four-poster bed, with the once elaborate canopy and drapes, giving the bed a majestic air.

Edinburgh, Holyrood Palace, The Front Entrance 1897 39169
The building of Holyroodhouse was started in about 1500 by James IV; the work continued under James V, who added a new tower and quadrangle. In May 1544, the palace was badly damaged when it was set on fire by the Earl of Hertford's troops.

Edinburgh, Holyroodhouse, The Chapel Front 1897 39170
This photograph shows the Chapel Royal at Holyroodhouse. It was originally the nave of the abbey founded in 1128 by David I.

Edinburgh, Holyroodhouse, The Remains of the Chapel Royal 1897 39171
The chapel was the burial place of David II, James II and James V. The chapel was sacked during the revolution of 1688, but the real damage was done in 1768 when the roof collapsed.

Edinburgh, St Giles's Cathedral 1897 39126
The High Kirk of St Giles was largely built in the 14th and 15th centuries. The tower, which dates from c1495, is topped off with what is considered to be the finest example of a crown steeple in the whole of Scotland.

▼ **Edinburgh, The Canongate Tolbooth c1890** E24503
The Canongate was where the canons of Holyrood Abbey entered the
Old Town. The tolbooth, with its projecting clock, is one of the most
famous landmarks on the Royal Mile and dates from 1591.

▼ **Edinburgh, The Canongate Tolbooth 1897** 39124A
In the great days of the Old Town, Canongate Street was where members of the Scottish aristocracy had their town houses.

▲ **Edinburgh,
Holyroodhouse and
Arthur's Seat c1900**
E24502
The dominating mass of
Arthur's seat, 822 ft high,
stands in a 648-acre
park.

◄ **Edinburgh, St Giles's Cathedral 1897** 39127
In 1634, Charles I attempted to re-establish the Scottish Episcopal Church, and St Giles's was for a short period elevated to the status of a cathedral. It became a cathedral again under Charles II, only to revert to being a parish church in 1688.

Edinburgh, St Giles's Cathedral 1897 39129
The oldest parish church in Edinburgh, St Giles's was erected in the early 12th century on the site of an older building. In 1385, much of the church was badly damaged by fire, and the rebuilding was not completed until 1460.

Edinburgh, St Giles's Cathedral 1897 39128
During the Reformation, the interior of the church was defaced, and altars and relics were destroyed. In 1559, John Knox was appointed minister of St Giles's. The building was in fact divided into four separate churches, and remained so until the 19th century.

Edinburgh, St Giles's Cathedral, The Tomb of the Marquis of Montrose 1897 39130
In 1644, James Graham, 5th Earl of Montrose, raised an army to fight for King Charles I. Against all odds,
Montrose gained victory after victory until his luck finally ran out at Philliphaugh in September 1645. Montrose
escaped to the Continent, but returned to raise troops for Charles II. Betrayed to the Covenanters, he was hung,
drawn and quartered at Edinburgh on 21 May 1650.

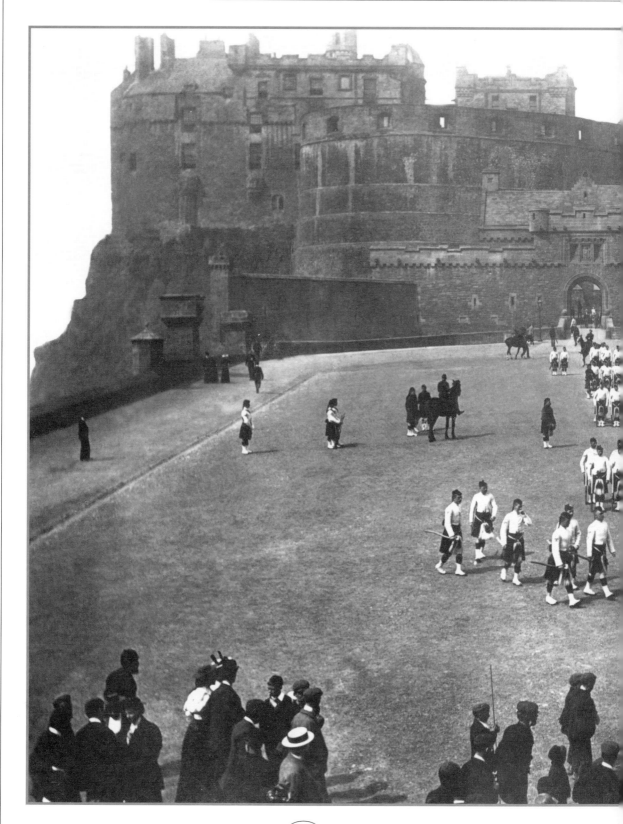

Edinburgh, The Castle 1897 39121a
A battalion of the Black Watch parade on the castle esplanade. Raised by General Wade in 1725, the Black Watch was formally constituted as a regiment of the line in 1739, and its strength was increased from four to ten companies.

Edinburgh, The Castle from the Grassmarket 1883

E24303

The grassmarket was the scene in 1736 of the Porteous Riots. A temporary gallows had been erected for the execution of Andrew Wilson for smuggling. Captain 'Black Jock' Porteous was in command of the city guard that took Wilson to his execution. A disturbance broke out, and Porteous ordered his men to open fire on the crowd. He was later arrested, tried and condemned to death; but because of the circumstances of the case, a stay of execution was granted until the king returned from Hanover. There were many people in Edinburgh who hated Porteous; fearing that he would be pardoned, a mob broke into the jail, hauled him off to the Grassmarket and lynched him. Despite the offering of a large reward for information, no one was ever charged with Porteous's murder.

◀ **Edinburgh, The Castle, The Cannon 'Mons Meg' c1950**

E24001

The cannon 'Mons Meg' is said to have been cast at Mons, Belgium in 1486, on the orders of James III. When James IV came to use the brute at the siege of Norham Castle in 1497, it took an artillery train of 220 men and 90 horses to get 'Mons Meg' to the scene of the action.

Edinburgh, The Castle from Johnston Terrace 1897 39120
During the reign of James III, the king's brothers were imprisoned here on suspicion of conspiring against him. John, Earl of Mar, died in Craigmillar Castle after being over-bled whilst suffering from a fever. Alexander, Duke of Albany, managed to kill his gaolers and escaped down a rope made of sheets.

Edinburgh, The Castle from Princes Gardens 1897 39119
The gardens, the railway line and Princes Street occupy the area once covered by the waters of Nor' Loch. The loch and an area of marshland formed a part of the castle's defences, but they also inhibited Edinburgh's expansion. The decision was taken in the 1770s to drain the loch and marshland to allow the development of the New Town.

Edinburgh, The Castle and the National Gallery 1897 E24506
The Edinburgh Castle we see today is, with a few additions, that built by the Earl of Morton following the siege of 1572. Morton succeeded Lennox as Regent, and took the fortress in the name of the infant James VI from the supporters of Mary, Queen of Scots. It was Morton who added the great half-moon battery to the castle's defences.

Edinburgh, The Castle from the Grassmarket 1897

39121

The site of the Marquis of Montrose's execution was not here, but at the Mercat Cross in the High Street. Having been declared a traitor in 1644, Montrose was not given the benefit of a trial. After hanging for three hours, his body was taken down and quartered. His head was set upon the tolbooth, and his limbs were sent for public display on the gates of Stirling, Glasgow, Perth and Aberdeen. In 1661, Montrose was allowed a state burial.

Edinburgh, A View from the Castle 1897 39101
In the foreground are the buildings of the Royal Institute and the National Gallery, with Princes Street on the left behind the Scott Monument. Calton Hill can be seen in the distance.

Edinburgh, The City and the Firth of Forth c1950 E24003
A tramcar rattles over the junction of Frederick Street and Princes Street. Edinburgh was well served by its tramway system for 85 years; services came to an end in November 1956.

Edinburgh, The University 1897 39134
Edinburgh University was founded by James VI in 1582. The buildings we see in this photograph were constructed between 1789 and 1827, and the dome was added in 1887. By the early years of the 20th century, the University had 3,000 students, 40 professors, 43 lecturers and 44 examiners.

Edinburgh, A View from the Castle c1950 E24004
A similar view to photograph No 39101, but separated in time by 50 years.

▼ **Edinburgh, Heriot's Hospital 1897** 39135
George Heriot, goldsmith and banker to James VI, founded the hospital.
He was immortalised as Jingling Geordie in Walter Scott's 'Fortunes of
Nigel'. Construction began on the hospital in 1628, but it was not com-
pleted until 1693 when it saw service as a military hospital.

▼ **Edinburgh, The Infirmary 1897** 39133
Built in the Scottish Baronial style, at a cost of £400,000, the infirmary
was dealing with 8,000 patients a year by 1900.

▲ **Edinburgh, The
Museum of Antiquities
1897** 39115
Founded in 1823, this
building, at the foot of
The Mound, housed a
statue gallery when this
picture was taken. There
was also a collection of
casts that was open only
to art students.

◀ **Edinburgh, Donaldson's Hospital 1897** 39136
The hospital was erected and endowed for the maintenance and education of up to 300 children, of whom 100 had speech and/or hearing difficulties. The benefactor was a wealthy printer who died in 1880, leaving £200,000 for the project.

Edinburgh, Waterloo Place 1897 39117
In the background on Calton Hill stands the unfinished monument to the Scottish dead of the Napoleonic Wars. The monument was started in 1822, but the money ran out and it was never completed.

Edinburgh, The National Gallery 1897 39106
The collection included paintings of the Spanish and Italian Schools, and the British were represented by artists such as Gainsborough. The annual Exhibition of the Scottish Academy was one of the highlights of the year.

Edinburgh, Princes Street, Looking West 1897 39107
It was possible to keep healthy on Princes Street. The Edinburgh Cafe at number 70 did not serve alcohol, and there was a Turkish baths at number 90. For those with a sweet tooth, Edinburgh rock was available at Ferguson's.

Edinburgh, The Museum and Castle 1900 E24509
The magnificent entrance to the Royal Institution.

Edinburgh, from Calton Hill 1897 39103A
In the foreground is the castellated bulk of the prison. The old Calton burial ground just beyond is where the philosopher David Hume is buried.

Edinburgh, Waterloo Place 1897 39116
On the left is the Register House containing the Scottish archives. Over on the right is the general post office. The statue is of the Duke of Wellington.

Edinburgh, The Scott Memorial 1897 39112
In this view of the Scott Memorial, we can see in the foreground a nanny enjoying a well earned rest.

Edinburgh, Princes Street 1897 39112A
Note the cabs and brakes alongside the Scott Monument. During the summer, excursions could be taken from here to the Forth Bridge and Queensferry and also to Roslin.

Edinburgh, Princes Street and the Scott Monument c1900 E24504
Princes Street and the Scott Monument from another part of the gardens.

Edinburgh, Princes Street 1897 39108
At the turn of the 20th century Princes Street boasted a number of hotels. The most expensive to stay at was the North British at Waverley Station. Next on the list were the Caledonian, the Station and the Royal, followed by the somewhat cheaper Royal British, the Douglas and the Bedford. There was also the Old Waverley, which was a temperance establishment.

Edinburgh, Princes Street, West End 1897 39113
Considered to be one of the finest boulevards in Europe, Princes Street was the place to shop and eat. Restaurants included a branch of Ferguson & Forrester, the Royal British, and Littlejohn's. Confectioners included Mackies, and also Ritchies, where shortbread was a speciality.

◀ **Edinburgh, Princes Street 1897** 39114
This photograph shows the junction of Hope Street, Queensferry Street and Sandwick Street. St John's and St Cuthbert's Churches, along with the castle, provide the backdrop.

◄ **Edinburgh, The Scott Monument and Princes Street Gardens c1900** E24510
The monument was designed by George Kemp and built between 1840 and 1844. Scott owned several houses in the city: the most famous was 39 Castle Street, where he wrote many of the Waverley novels.

▼ **Edinburgh, Waverley Station 1833** E24302
The platform canopies were still under construction when this photograph was taken. The station was originally called North Bridge, but it was renamed in April 1866.

◄ **Edinburgh, Princes Gardens 1897** 39122
This view of Princes Gardens looks towards The Mound.

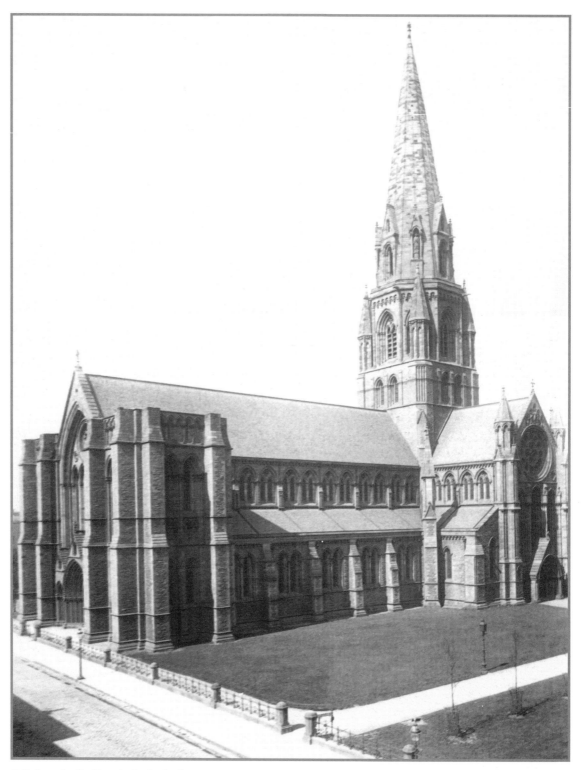

Edinburgh, St Mary's Cathedral 1897 39131
Designed by Sir Gilbert Scott, construction began in 1874 and was finally completed in 1917.

Edinburgh, St Mary's Cathedral 1897 39132
Here we see the imposing interior of St Mary's Cathedral. By 1879, construction costs amounted to more than £110,000.

Roslin

Roslin is famous for its castle and chapel. The oldest part of the castle, which was founded by Sir William Sinclair, dates from the early 14th century. The consecration of the chapel was delayed because a murder had been committed on the premises by the chief stonemason.

Roslin Chapel 1897 39164
The chapel, which is famed for its elaborate carvings, was founded in 1446 as a collegiate church, but only the lady chapel and choir were completed. The church was badly damaged by rioters in 1688 and was restored in the 19th century.

Roslin, The Castle from the Glen 1897 39167
The castle stands on a cliff above the river North Esk. The oldest part dates from the early 14th century. It was enlarged in the 1440s.

Roslin Castle 1897 39166
All but destroyed in 1544 during an English invasion, the castle was rebuilt by 1580. Further additions were made during the 17th century.

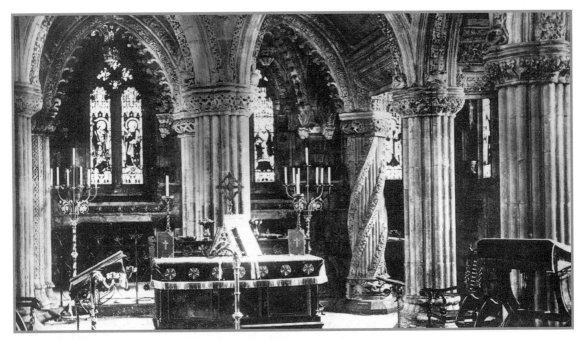

Roslin Chapel, Interior 1897 39164a
The chapel is famed for its pillar of entwined ribbands. The story is that the chief stonemason went to Italy to study a similar pillar. While he was away, his apprentice worked out how to construct the pillar after having a dream and built it. On his return, the mason was so jealous of his apprentice's work that he struck the boy dead.

Roslin Castle, Part of the Old Ruins 1897 39165
The castle and church have long been popular with tourists, many of whom stay to sample the delights of the Old Rosslyn Inn. Among those to imbibe have been Johnson and Boswell in 1773, Robert Burns, Queen Victoria and Edward VII.

Hawthornden

Located nine miles south of Edinburgh, Hawthornden stands high above the river North Esk amid a densely wooded estate. The home of the poet William Drummond (1585-1649), the house was extensively rebuilt by him in 1638.

Hawthornden 1897 39159
The English poet laureate Ben Jonson stayed here from December 1618 until the middle of January 1619 as a guest of William Drummond.

Hawthornden, From the Glen 1897 39161
A picturesque view of Hawthornden.

Hawthornden, The Courtyard 1897 39163
Jonson was 45 years old when in 1618 he left London and walked the 400 miles to Scotland. At Darlington his shoes gave out, and he had to buy another pair. He later told Drummond that they took some breaking in and left his feet sore and blistered for several days.

Hawthornden, Ben Jonson's Tree 1897 39162
It is said that Drummond was sitting under the great sycamore tree in front of the house when Jonson trudged up the path. Drummond met him with 'Welcome, welcome, royal Ben!' Jonson replied: 'Thank ye, thank ye, Hawthornden! Drummond's library was one of the finest of its day, containing about 1,400 books in English, French, Latin, Greek, Spanish, Italian and Hebrew.

North Berwick

It was at North Berwick, in 1591, that the devil is said to have appeared to a group of witches in St Andrew's Kirk. At their trial for witchcraft, the women confessed that they not only knew the most intimate secrets of the king's bedchamber, but that their satanic leader was none other than Francis Stewart, Earl of Bothwell. Bothwell, though well-educated, was probably mad, and not afraid of using violence. The king, who believed in witchcraft, ordered Bothwell's arrest. Bothwell escaped from custody and crossed into England, only to return at Christmas and attack Holyroodhouse, threatening to torch the place. It was almost certainly the intervention of some of the local citizens that saved the situation from getting completely out of hand. An attempt by Bothwell to kidnap James was botched; but not to be outdone, the earl descended once more upon Holyroodhouse, demanding a trial for witchcraft. Bothwell never got his trial. He left Scotland, and eventually died in poverty at Naples.

North Berwick, Quality Street 1897 39176
The corner shop is long gone, but the clock tower remains.

▼ **North Berwick 1897** 39183
Tourism brought with it a spate of hotel-building. The Royal was joined by the impressive Marine Hotel which had hot and cold running water.

▼ **North Berwick, The Law 1897** 39175
North Berwick Law rises 612 ft above the town. On the summit is a watch-tower dating from the Napoleonic Wars, and an archway made from the jawbones of a whale.

▲ **North Berwick, The Marine Hotel and the Links 1897** 39177
North Berwick's popularity as a resort began in the 1840s, but as late as 1859, when HRH The Prince of Wales visited the town, there was a serious lack of accommodation for tourists. The project to build a hotel somehow became involved with plans for a new gas works under the North Berwick Hotel & Gas Company.

◀ **North Berwick, The Seafront 1897** 39180
The popular seafront of North Berwick.

North Berwick, The Bay 1897 39179
Here we see the broad sweep of the sandy bay to the east of the harbour area on a quiet day.

Tantallon Castle 1897
39187
The Douglases were a powerful family: they were wardens of the Border Marches, lords of Galloway and skilled in war. By the end of the 15th century they controlled vast areas including Galloway, Lothian, Stirlingshire and Clydesdale.

Tantallon Castle 1897 39184

In 1388, the 2nd Earl of Douglas invaded the Earl of Northumberland's domain to the south. Douglas raided far and wide; then, after capturing Northumberland's standard, he returned home. On 5 August 1388, the two sides clashed yet again. In the savage hand-to-hand fighting that went on all night Douglas was killed, and the Earl of Northumberland was taken prisoner.

The Bass Rock 1897 39188

One of the more interesting events in the history of this famous bird sanctuary occurred after the Battle of Killicrankie in July 1689. Despite defeating the forces of William III, the Jacobites failed to hold the advantage. One of the outcomes was that the Bass Rock was taken and held in the name of James VII from June 1691 to April 1694.

Tantallon Castle 1897 39186
James V was resentful of the Douglases, so he laid siege to Tantallon in 1528. Red Douglas held out for three weeks before surrendering. Douglas went into exile in England, and his estates were forfeited to the crown.

Tyninghame House, The Ladies' Walk 1897 39181
Here we see the finely wooded grounds of Tyninghame House, the seat of the Earl of Haddington; the grounds were open to the public on Saturdays.

Whitekirk

The village and church probably owe their existence to the discovery of a holy well in 1294. Aeneas Sylvius Piccolomini (later Pope Pius II) came here during the reign of James I.

Left: **Whitekirk, The Village c1955** W3275002
A view of the village of Whitekirk.

Below: **Whitekirk, St Mary's Church c1955**
W3275001
Here we see the 15th-century cruciform church of St Mary's, its massive tower surmounted by a wooden spire. The church was targeted by the suffragettes during a campaign of violence following the government's refusal to grant votes for women. Other targets for fire-bombing included Farrington Hall and Leuchars railway station.

Blackburn

Sandwiched between Whitburn and Livingston, Blackburn in West Lothian stands on the River Almond. This selection of pictures were taken at the beginning of the 1960s.

Blackburn, The Centre c1960 B7585008
A bleak featureless view of Blackburn New Town.

Blackburn, The Centre and the Bowling Green c1960 B7585009
Typical 1960s structures span the whole photograph. This was the typical layout of a 1960s new town.

Blackburn, The River Almond and Hopefield Bridge c1960 B7585006
The River Almond flows into the Firth of Forth at Cramond. A prophetess at Cramond is said to have warned James
I of impending tragedy if he continued with his journey to Perth. He was murdered.

Blackburn, The Shopping Centre and the Golden Hind Hotel c1960 B7585004
The precinct is typical of a style that dominated redevelopment and new town schemes of the late 1950s and 1960s. Examples can be seen throughout the UK, many of them now looking the worse for wear.

Blackburn, The Almondvale 'Old Folks' Home c1960 B7585002
Again, this building is typical of the 1960s. Everything looks unused in this photograph, the 'Old folks' home looks unloved in as yet, and the trees seem to have been just planted.

Blackburn, The River Almond c1960
B7585005
The River Almond flows from Blackburn to the three towns of East, Mid and West Calder. It was at Mid Calder in 1556 that John Knox first administered Communion according to Protestant rites.

Index

Frith Book Co Titles

www.francisfrith.co.uk

The Frith Book Company publishes over 100 new titles each year. A selection of those currently available are listed below. For latest catalogue please contact Frith Book Co.

Town Books 96 pages, approx 100 photos. County and Themed Books 128 pages, approx 150 photos (unless specified). All titles hardback laminated case and jacket except those indicated pb (paperback)

Amersham, Chesham & Rickmansworth (pb)			Derby (pb)	1-85937-367-4	£9.99
	1-85937-340-2	£9.99	Derbyshire (pb)	1-85937-196-5	£9.99
Ancient Monuments & Stone Circles	1-85937-143-4	£17.99	Devon (pb)	1-85937-297-x	£9.99
Aylesbury (pb)	1-85937-227-9	£9.99	Dorset (pb)	1-85937-269-4	£9.99
Bakewell	1-85937-113-2	£12.99	Dorset Churches	1-85937-172-8	£17.99
Barnstaple (pb)	1-85937-300-3	£9.99	Dorset Coast (pb)	1-85937-299-6	£9.99
Bath (pb)	1-85937-419-0	£9.99	Dorset Living Memories	1-85937-210-4	£14.99
Bedford (pb)	1-85937-205-8	£9.99	Down the Severn	1-85937-118-3	£14.99
Berkshire (pb)	1-85937-191-4	£9.99	Down the Thames (pb)	1-85937-278-3	£9.99
Berkshire Churches	1-85937-170-1	£17.99	Down the Trent	1-85937-311-9	£14.99
Blackpool (pb)	1-85937-382-8	£9.99	Dublin (pb)	1-85937-231-7	£9.99
Bognor Regis (pb)	1-85937-431-x	£9.99	East Anglia (pb)	1-85937-265-1	£9.99
Bournemouth	1-85937-067-5	£12.99	East London	1-85937-080-2	£14.99
Bradford (pb)	1-85937-204-x	£9.99	East Sussex	1-85937-130-2	£14.99
Brighton & Hove(pb)	1-85937-192-2	£8.99	Eastbourne	1-85937-061-6	£12.99
Bristol (pb)	1-85937-264-3	£9.99	Edinburgh (pb)	1-85937-193-0	£8.99
British Life A Century Ago (pb)	1-85937-213-9	£9.99	England in the 1880s	1-85937-331-3	£17.99
Buckinghamshire (pb)	1-85937-200-7	£9.99	English Castles (pb)	1-85937-434-4	£9.99
Camberley (pb)	1-85937-222-8	£9.99	English Country Houses	1-85937-161-2	£17.99
Cambridge (pb)	1-85937-422-0	£9.99	Essex (pb)	1-85937-270-8	£9.99
Cambridgeshire (pb)	1-85937-420-4	£9.99	Exeter	1-85937-126-4	£12.99
Canals & Waterways (pb)	1-85937-291-0	£9.99	Exmoor	1-85937-132-9	£14.99
Canterbury Cathedral (pb)	1-85937-179-5	£9.99	Falmouth	1-85937-066-7	£12.99
Cardiff (pb)	1-85937-093-4	£9.99	Folkestone (pb)	1-85937-124-8	£9.99
Carmarthenshire	1-85937-216-3	£14.99	Glasgow (pb)	1-85937-190-6	£9.99
Chelmsford (pb)	1-85937-310-0	£9.99	Gloucestershire	1-85937-102-7	£14.99
Cheltenham (pb)	1-85937-095-0	£9.99	Great Yarmouth (pb)	1-85937-426-3	£9.99
Cheshire (pb)	1-85937-271-6	£9.99	Greater Manchester (pb)	1-85937-266-x	£9.99
Chester	1-85937-090-x	£12.99	Guildford (pb)	1-85937-410-7	£9.99
Chesterfield	1-85937-378-x	£9.99	Hampshire (pb)	1-85937-279-1	£9.99
Chichester (pb)	1-85937-228-7	£9.99	Hampshire Churches (pb)	1-85937-207-4	£9.99
Colchester (pb)	1-85937-188-4	£8.99	Harrogate	1-85937-423-9	£9.99
Cornish Coast	1-85937-163-9	£14.99	Hastings & Bexhill (pb)	1-85937-131-0	£9.99
Cornwall (pb)	1-85937-229-5	£9.99	Heart of Lancashire (pb)	1-85937-197-3	£9.99
Cornwall Living Memories	1-85937-248-1	£14.99	Helston (pb)	1-85937-214-7	£9.99
Cotswolds (pb)	1-85937-230-9	£9.99	Hereford (pb)	1-85937-175-2	£9.99
Cotswolds Living Memories	1-85937-255-4	£14.99	Herefordshire	1-85937-174-4	£14.99
County Durham	1-85937-123-x	£14.99	Hertfordshire (pb)	1-85937-247-3	£9.99
Croydon Living Memories	1-85937-162-0	£9.99	Horsham (pb)	1-85937-432-8	£9.99
Cumbria	1-85937-101-9	£14.99	Humberside	1-85937-215-5	£14.99
Dartmoor	1-85937-145-0	£14.99	Hythe, Romney Marsh & Ashford	1-85937-256-2	£9.99

Available from your local bookshop or from the publisher

Frith Book Co Titles (continued)

Ipswich (pb)	1-85937-424-7	£9.99	St Ives (pb)	1-85937415-8	£9.99
Ireland (pb)	1-85937-181-7	£9.99	Scotland (pb)	1-85937-182-5	£9.99
Isle of Man (pb)	1-85937-268-6	£9.99	Scottish Castles (pb)	1-85937-323-2	£9.99
Isles of Scilly	1-85937-136-1	£14.99	Sevenoaks & Tunbridge	1-85937-057-8	£12.99
Isle of Wight (pb)	1-85937-429-8	£9.99	Sheffield, South Yorks (pb)	1-85937-267-8	£9.99
Isle of Wight Living Memories	1-85937-304-6	£14.99	Shrewsbury (pb)	1-85937-325-9	£9.99
Kent (pb)	1-85937-189-2	£9.99	Shropshire (pb)	1-85937-326-7	£9.99
Kent Living Memories	1-85937-125-6	£14.99	Somerset	1-85937-153-1	£14.99
Lake District (pb)	1-85937-275-9	£9.99	South Devon Coast	1-85937-107-8	£14.99
Lancaster, Morecambe & Heysham (pb)	1-85937-233-3	£9.99	South Devon Living Memories	1-85937-168-x	£14.99
Leeds (pb)	1-85937-202-3	£9.99	South Hams	1-85937-220-1	£14.99
Leicester	1-85937-073-x	£12.99	Southampton (pb)	1-85937-427-1	£9.99
Leicestershire (pb)	1-85937-185-x	£9.99	Southport (pb)	1-85937-425-5	£9.99
Lincolnshire (pb)	1-85937-433-6	£9.99	Staffordshire	1-85937-047-0	£12.99
Liverpool & Merseyside (pb)	1-85937-234-1	£9.99	Stratford upon Avon	1-85937-098-5	£12.99
London (pb)	1-85937-183-3	£9.99	Suffolk (pb)	1-85937-221-x	£9.99
Ludlow (pb)	1-85937-176-0	£9.99	Suffolk Coast	1-85937-259-7	£14.99
Luton (pb)	1-85937-235-x	£9.99	Surrey (pb)	1-85937-240-6	£9.99
Maidstone	1-85937-056-x	£14.99	Sussex (pb)	1-85937-184-1	£9.99
Manchester (pb)	1-85937-198-1	£9.99	Swansea (pb)	1-85937-167-1	£9.99
Middlesex	1-85937-158-2	£14.99	Tees Valley & Cleveland	1-85937-211-2	£14.99
New Forest	1-85937-128-0	£14.99	Thanet (pb)	1-85937-116-7	£9.99
Newark (pb)	1-85937-366-6	£9.99	Tiverton (pb)	1-85937-178-7	£9.99
Newport, Wales (pb)	1-85937-258-9	£9.99	Torbay	1-85937-063-2	£12.99
Newquay (pb)	1-85937-421-2	£9.99	Truro	1-85937-147-7	£12.99
Norfolk (pb)	1-85937-195-7	£9.99	Victorian and Edwardian Cornwall	1-85937-252-x	£14.99
Norfolk Living Memories	1-85937-217-1	£14.99	Victorian & Edwardian Devon	1-85937-253-8	£14.99
Northamptonshire	1-85937-150-7	£14.99	Victorian & Edwardian Kent	1-85937-149-3	£14.99
Northumberland Tyne & Wear (pb)	1-85937-281-3	£9.99	Vic & Ed Maritime Album	1-85937-144-2	£17.99
North Devon Coast	1-85937-146-9	£14.99	Victorian and Edwardian Sussex	1-85937-157-4	£14.99
North Devon Living Memories	1-85937-261-9	£14.99	Victorian & Edwardian Yorkshire	1-85937-154-x	£14.99
North London	1-85937-206-6	£14.99	Victorian Seaside	1-85937-159-0	£17.99
North Wales (pb)	1-85937-298-8	£9.99	Villages of Devon (pb)	1-85937-293-7	£9.99
North Yorkshire (pb)	1-85937-236-8	£9.99	Villages of Kent (pb)	1-85937-294-5	£9.99
Norwich (pb)	1-85937-194-9	£8.99	Villages of Sussex (pb)	1-85937-295-3	£9.99
Nottingham (pb)	1-85937-324-0	£9.99	Warwickshire (pb)	1-85937-203-1	£9.99
Nottinghamshire (pb)	1-85937-187-6	£9.99	Welsh Castles (pb)	1-85937-322-4	£9.99
Oxford (pb)	1-85937-411-5	£9.99	West Midlands (pb)	1-85937-289-9	£9.99
Oxfordshire (pb)	1-85937-430-1	£9.99	West Sussex	1-85937-148-5	£14.99
Peak District (pb)	1-85937-280-5	£9.99	West Yorkshire (pb)	1-85937-201-5	£9.99
Penzance	1-85937-069-1	£12.99	Weymouth (pb)	1-85937-209-0	£9.99
Peterborough (pb)	1-85937-219-8	£9.99	Wiltshire (pb)	1-85937-277-5	£9.99
Piers	1-85937-237-6	£17.99	Wiltshire Churches (pb)	1-85937-171-x	£9.99
Plymouth	1-85937-119-1	£12.99	Wiltshire Living Memories	1-85937-245-7	£14.99
Poole & Sandbanks (pb)	1-85937-251-1	£9.99	Winchester (pb)	1-85937-428-x	£9.99
Preston (pb)	1-85937-212-0	£9.99	Windmills & Watermills	1-85937-242-2	£17.99
Reading (pb)	1-85937-238-4	£9.99	Worcester (pb)	1-85937-165-5	£9.99
Romford (pb)	1-85937-319-4	£9.99	Worcestershire	1-85937-152-3	£14.99
Salisbury (pb)	1-85937-239-2	£9.99	York (pb)	1-85937-199-x	£9.99
Scarborough (pb)	1-85937-379-8	£9.99	Yorkshire (pb)	1-85937-186-8	£9.99
St Albans (pb)	1-85937-341-0	£9.99	Yorkshire Living Memories	1-85937-166-3	£14.99

See Frith books on the internet www.francisfrith.co.uk

FRITH PRODUCTS & SERVICES

Francis Frith would doubtless be pleased to know that the pioneering publishing venture he started in 1860 still continues today. A hundred and forty years later, The Francis Frith Collection continues in the same innovative tradition and is now one of the foremost publishers of vintage photographs in the world. Some of the current activities include:

Interior Decoration

Today Frith's photographs can be seen framed and as giant wall murals in thousands of pubs, restaurants, hotels, banks, retail stores and other public buildings throughout the country. In every case they enhance the unique local atmosphere of the places they depict and provide reminders of gentler days in an increasingly busy and frenetic world.

Product Promotions

Frith products are used by many major companies to promote the sales of their own products or to reinforce their own history and heritage. Frith promotions have been used by Hovis bread, Courage beers, Scots Porage Oats, Colman's mustard, Cadbury's foods, Mellow Birds coffee, Dunhill pipe tobacco, Guinness, and Bulmer's Cider.

Genealogy and Family History

As the interest in family history and roots grows world-wide, more and more people are turning to Frith's photographs of Great Britain for images of the towns, villages and streets where their ancestors lived; and, of course, photographs of the churches and chapels where their ancestors were christened, married and buried are an essential part of every genealogy tree and family album.

Frith Products

All Frith photographs are available Framed or just as Mounted Prints and Posters (size 23 x 16 inches). These may be ordered from the address below. From time to time other products - Address Books, Calendars, Table Mats, etc - are available.

The Internet

Already twenty thousand Frith photographs can be viewed and purchased on the internet through the Frith websites and a myriad of partner sites.

For more detailed information on Frith companies and products, look at these sites:

www.francisfrith.co.uk
www.francisfrith.com
(for North American visitors)

See the complete list of Frith Books at:

www.francisfrith.co.uk

This web site is regularly updated with the latest list of publications from the Frith Book Company. If you wish to buy books relating to another part of the country that your local bookshop does not stock, you may purchase on-line.

For further information, trade, or author enquiries please contact us at the address below:
The Francis Frith Collection, Frith's Barn, Teffont, Salisbury, Wiltshire, England SP3 5QP.
Tel: +44 (0)1722 716 376 Fax: +44 (0)1722 716 881   Email: sales@francisfrith.co.uk

See Frith books on the internet www.francisfrith.co.uk

TO RECEIVE YOUR FREE MOUNTED PRINT

Mounted Print
Overall size 14 x 11 inches

Cut out this Voucher and return it with your remittance for £1.95 to cover postage and handling, to UK addresses. For overseas addresses please include £4.00 post and handling. Choose any photograph included in this book. Your SEPIA print will be A4 in size, and mounted in a cream mount with burgundy rule line, overall size 14 x 11 inches.

Order additional Mounted Prints at HALF PRICE (only £7.49 each*)

If there are further pictures you would like to order, possibly as gifts for friends and family, purchase them at half price (no additional postage and handling required).

Have your Mounted Prints framed*

For an additional £14.95 per print you can have your chosen Mounted Print framed in an elegant polished wood and gilt moulding, overall size 16 x 13 inches (no additional postage and handling required).

> *** IMPORTANT!**
> These special prices are only available if ordered using the original voucher on this page (no copies permitted) and at the same time as your free Mounted Print, for delivery to the same address

Frith Collectors' Guild

From time to time we publish a magazine of news and stories about Frith photographs and further special offers of Frith products. If you would like 12 months FREE membership, please return this form.

Send completed forms to:
The Francis Frith Collection, Frith's Barn, Teffont, Salisbury, Wiltshire SP3 5QP

Voucher for FREE and Reduced Price Frith Prints

Picture no.	Page number	Qty	Mounted @ £7.49	Framed + £14.95	Total Cost
		1	**Free of charge***	£	£
			£7.49	£	£
			£7.49	£	£
			£7.49	£	£
			£7.49	£	£
			£7.49	£	£

Please allow 28 days for delivery	*** Post & handling**	**£1.95**
Book Title	**Total Order Cost**	**£**

Please do not photocopy this voucher. Only the original is valid, so please cut it out and return it to us.

I enclose a cheque / postal order for £ . . . . made payable to 'The Francis Frith Collection' OR please debit my Mastercard / Visa / Switch / Amex card *(credit cards please on all overseas orders)*

Number . . . .

Issue No(Switch only) . . . . .Valid from (Amex/Switch) . . . .

Expires . . . . Signature . . . .

Name Mr/Mrs/Ms . . . .

Address . . . .

. . . .

. . . . Postcode . . . .

Daytime Tel No . . . .   Valid to 31/12/02

The Francis Frith Collectors' Guild

Please enrol me as a member for 12 months free of charge.

Name Mr/Mrs/Ms . . . .

Address . . . .

. . . .

. . . . Postcode . . . .

Would you like to find out more about Francis Frith?

We have recently recruited some entertaining speakers who are happy to visit local groups, clubs and societies to give an illustrated talk documenting Frith's travels and photographs. If you are a member of such a group and are interested in hosting a presentation, we would love to hear from you.

Our speakers bring with them a small selection of our local town and county books, together with sample prints. They are happy to take orders. A small proportion of the order value is donated to the group who have hosted the presentation. The talks are therefore an excellent way of fundraising for small groups and societies.

Can you help us with information about any of the Frith photographs in this book?

We are gradually compiling an historical record for each of the photographs in the Frith archive. It is always fascinating to find out the names of the people shown in the pictures, as well as insights into the shops, buildings and other features depicted.

If you recognize anyone in the photographs in this book, or if you have information not already included in the author's caption, do let us know. We would love to hear from you, and will try to publish it in future books or articles.

Our production team

Frith books are produced by a small dedicated team at offices in the converted Grade II listed 18th-century barn at Teffont near Salisbury, illustrated above. Most have worked with the Frith Collection for many years. All have in common one quality: they have a passion for the Frith Collection. The team is constantly expanding, but currently includes:

Jason Buck, John Buck, Douglas Burns, Heather Crisp, Isobel Hall, Rob Hames, Hazel Heaton, Peter Horne, James Kinnear, Tina Leary, Hannah Marsh, Eliza Sackett, Terence Sackett, Sandra Sanger, Shelley Tolcher, Susanna Walker, Clive Wathen and Jenny Wathen.

Free Print – see overleaf